This book belongs to:

_____

_____

A catalogue record for this book is available
from the British Library

Published by Ladybird Books Ltd
80 Strand London WC2R 0RL
A Penguin Company

© Disney MMI

Based on the Pooh stories by

A.A Milne (copyright The Pooh Properties Trust)

LADYBIRD and the device of a Ladybird are trademarks
of Ladybird Books Ltd

Too much honey

Ladybird

honey

Christopher
Robin

Kanga

Roo

Eeyore

Pooh

tree

Rabbit

Gopher

Winnie the Pooh was sad.
There was no honey in
his honeypot.

So Pooh went to
Rabbit's house.

 7

Pooh pulled himself into
Rabbit's house.

He ate Rabbit's honey.

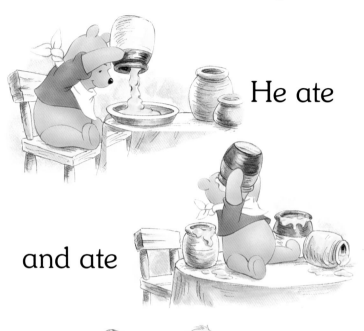

He ate

and ate

and ate.

 9

When all the honey was
gone, Pooh stopped.

Then he pulled himself
out of Rabbit's house.

He pulled and pulled and
pulled. But Pooh was stuck.

Rabbit pushed Pooh.

He pushed and pushed
and pushed. But Pooh
was stuck.

Along came Christopher
Robin.
"I am stuck," said Pooh.
"Can you get me out?"

RABBIT'S
HOUSE

Christopher Robin pulled
Pooh and Rabbit pulled
Christopher Robin.
They pulled and pulled and
pulled. But Pooh was stuck.

"You will have to wait,"
said Christopher Robin.

Pooh waited and waited
and waited.

Along came Eeyore.
"I am stuck," said Pooh.
"Can you get me out?"

"No," said Eeyore. "You will have to wait."

Pooh waited and waited
and waited.

Along came Gopher.
"I am stuck," said Pooh.
"Can you get me out?"

"No," said Gopher. "You
will have to wait."

21

Pooh waited and waited…

and waited.

Along came Christopher
Robin, Rabbit, Eeyore,
Kanga and Roo.
"Now we can get you out,"
said Christopher Robin.

Christopher Robin and
Kanga and Eeyore and
Roo pulled Pooh.
They pulled and pulled
and pulled.

 24

Out popped Pooh.
He went up, up, up.

Pooh was stuck in
a honey tree.
"We will get you out,"
said Christopher Robin.

"I can wait!" said Pooh.